PUT YOUR MOUTH ON HIM

A Collection of Prayers and Affirmations

By: Dr. Sybil M. Sloan

TABLE OF CONTENTS

This book is dedicated to all of the men who has felt dishonored by the words spoken to them and over them.

Prayer Contributions by:

My Mother and National Vice Commander for NABVETS, Inc., Mary E. Elliott

and

Kathie L. Robinson

MY PURPOSE

I myself went through a season of my life where I spoke to men in a way that not only tore them down, but also caused them to question every part of their manhood. I caused injuries that not only hindered his effectiveness as a man, but it also caused long lasting injuries as it relates to being with another woman and serving God whole heartedly. I am not proud of the wounds I created or contributed to. I have made natural apologies to those men and I have prayed for their full restoration, through Christ. This book is my restitution and reminder that our men are here to reassure us and that cannot be done if they have been left unsure. Men being encouraged, edified and empowered is part of why I think God created me. Although I mishandled the gift initially God did not allow my ignorance to destroy me. I have in some instances used this gift inappropriately, but with age has come wisdom.

This book's symbolism is much like that of our hands. When a man or woman puts their hands on their mate, the abused mate has no comfort in the abuser using those same hands for the purpose of comfort. It takes, spiritual deliverance and in some instances therapy to move past the aftermath of abuse.

Ladies, once we use our mouths to tear a man down, most often, he no longer desires to hear anything come out of our mouths. James 3:10 says, "Blessings and Curses come out of the same mouth. My sisters surely this is not right." This book is not a sum total of how to speak to your mate; however, it is a solid foundation.

WHEN WAS THE LAST TIME YOU PUT YOUR MOUTH ON HIM?

Put Your Mouth on Him is a book birthed in a time and in a climate where men are being emasculated more than ever. This book is to encourage women to use words of life as they speak to and about their men. The woman's mouth is a powerful tool and she can use it on a man in ways that will cause his entire world to change. The Book of James in Chapter 3 speaks of not sinning with the tongue.

We pray this book helps each woman change the world of the man in her life, by reshaping his environment and increasing her positive energy in his world. This book is one of our ways to guide and demonstrate to every woman HOW to put her mouth on her man and cause him to RISE every time. Our intent is to help lead couples into multiple orgasmic encounters and create mental stimulation, which will lead to a more fulfilling physical stimulation.

It is our privilege and responsibility to speak in a way that urge and unction a man to perform better in every area of his life, overall. We challenge each couple that reads to this book to allow the mouth to explore areas mentally that has never been touched. Once we climax mentally this creates a desire to not just explore our mates' minds, but to explore their bodies as well. Hence addressing what majority say is one of the top 3 reasons for divorce.

HE WANTS TO BE THE PROVIDER

Many men are faced with the task of being the PROVIDER. Needless to say, a lot of men have a strong desire to feel needed. Men like to be our knights in shining armor. Therefore, he takes pride in rescuing the one he loves. Men understand that sometimes it does not look like what society has outlaid. When not properly esteemed and exhorted, men may begin to feel worthless and insignificant . This can also take place if we don't allow them to take the leading role.

Ladies, we were not created to be INDEPENDENT, do you know what I mean? Let's move away from this societal genocide of the family structure. We need men just as men need us. God ordained and established this from the foundations of the earth. We were not created to live independent of one another. Ladies we cannot continue to allow Corporate America to cause us to further emasculate our men. We cannot allow our divorced and miserable family and friends to encourage us to set a standard in a mate we are not worthy of or capable of reciprocating.

There are times that we make more money and that is okay. We should not allow our resources to cause us to weaken our men. We have to strategically and intentionally find a way to minister to him and make him feel like he has as much of a voice in the finances .

Sometimes, even when you know you are in control, make him feel like HE IS!!

SELF-TEST

(Sometimes we just have to check ourselves,
so we don't wreck ourselves.)

Ask yourself when was the last time you put your mouth on him?

When was the last time you caused him to rise to a place where he felt as if he could conquer any mountain?

When was the last time he told you he enjoyed your mouth?

Has he ever said he didn't want to hear your mouth? If so how many times?

Are you ready to PUT YOUR MOUTH ON HIM?

COLLECTION OF PRAYERS

GODLY MAN

Heavenly Father, thank you for this Godly man you have placed in my life. He has been anointed to lead our family. I know we came from different homes and maybe our parents even used two different approaches to parenting, but this man of God came into the world for Purpose. Father you have ordered his life since before the foundations of the earth. There is nothing that can be done to change the anointing and favor that has been placed upon his life. Father I know the Bible says in **Ezekiel 22:30 " I searched for a man among them who would build up the wall and stand in the gap before Me for the land so that would not**

destroy but, I could not find no one." Father I submit this a man who will stand in the gap, not only for his family, but for you God. Keep him covered from the crown of his head to the soles of his feet.

In Jesus Name, Amen.

Husband

Heavenly Father, I come to you humbly with gratitude, thanking you for the man of God you have allowed him to seek me and find me. The Bible says in **Proverbs 18:22, "he who finds a wife, finds a good thing and obtains favor from the Lord." Truly the favor of the Lord is upon my man of God."** Lord we know his journey to locating me has not been easy father, for I have been out of place for a long time. Lord redeem our time in the earth. Allow us the opportunity to have a lot of first-time experiences together as if we were in our youth. Father allow his wisdom to be increased. Remove any doubts he may have in his heart about starting over in a new relationship with intent of it being for a lifetime. Reshape our minds for covenant marriages. Remove any and all scales that cover our eyes and prevents us from seeing and manifesting all you have in store for us. Now father bind us together like only you can. Renew our love for you and each other daily. Cause us to be what we desire in the other. Remind us daily that he without sin is the only one that can cast a stone. Remind us that we will serve the Lord.

In Jesus Name, Amen.

PRAYER FOR A FATHER

Father (Abba) I thank you for fathers both natural and spiritual. I thank you for your compassion you placed in him according to your word in **Psalms 103:13, Like as a father pitieth his children, so the Lord pitieth them that fear him.** Abba I thank you that my father is a father that sings over me deliverance and provides protection and hiding from life's storms according to **Psalms 32:7-8 Thou art my hiding place; thou shalt preserve me from trouble; thou shalt compass me about with songs of deliverance. Selah.**

⁸ I will instruct thee and teach thee in the way which thou shalt go: I will guide thee with mine eye. Abba you placed wisdom in my father to show me a correct path without bringing a bad view of you Abba. My father rejoices in me when I'm righteous and according to **Proverbs 14:26 In the fear of the Lord is strong confidence: and his children shall have a place of refuge.** Father this is my secure fortress and refuge. Abba thank you for placing fathers that speak a blessing over me and not curses such as Jacob did over his sons. Thank you for fathers that are just in judgement as Moses was with the daughters of

Zelophehad. Abba because you are the "Good Father" I rest in the strategy of the fathers placed in my life.

We seal this prayer in mighty and matchless blood of Jesus the Christ.

PRAYERS FOR SON – 7 (SEVEN) DAYS

~ CONTRIBUTIONS BY MARY ELLIOTT

 Day One

Dear Lord, bless and keep my son with a strong mind and full of courage to choose the path of righteousness and a long life fulfilling your purpose, your word says in **Psalms 1:6 - For the LORD knoweth the way of the righteous: but the way of the ungodly shall perish.** Lord I decree with long life shall you satisfy him. Lord not just him, but the issue of his loins.

We ask these things in Christ name, Amen.

Day Two

Heavenly Father, please be a force around my son and help him to not be persuaded to make decisions that lead to destruction, but to overcome every Temptation – Help him to trust and "obey" your WORD in **Matthew 4:4 – But he answered and said, It is written, Man shall not live by bread alone, but by every word that proceedeth out of the mouth of God.** Now Father lead him not into temptation, but deliver him from all manners of evil, for thine is the. Kingdom and the Power and the Glory forever.

Amen.

DAY THREE

Dear Lord, thank you for the gift of a son – may your loving arms of protection surround him each day and let him know he is precious in your sight!! Thank you for the wisdom you have deposited in this vessel. Thank you for keeping his mind stayed on you. **Proverbs 10:1 – A wise son maketh a glad father: but a foolish son is the heaviness of his mother.**

You, son, brought joy to a heart that felt unfulfilled – continue to be that "one in a million" – keep your light shining. Jesus keep him safe! **Proverbs 7:1, 2 – My son, keep my words, and lay up my commandments with thee. 2 Keep my commandments, and live; and my law as the apple of thine eye.** Lord we consider all of these things done.

In Jesus Name, Amen.

Day Four

Praying Son, for you to always know you are loved by God and you are loved by me. Sometimes as a mother I have to correct you. I know it sometimes feels like I am riding you back, it is only because I love you and only want God's best for you. I do not want you to be the statistics that I read about daily – Hear my Prayer dear Lord and bring this request clear in his mind and heart! **Luke 2:25, 26 – And, behold, there was a man in Jerusalem, whose name was Simeon; and the same man was just and devout, waiting for the consolation of Israel: and the Holy Ghost was upon him. 26 And it was revealed unto him by the Holy Ghost, that he should not see death, before he had seen the Lord's Christ.** Father I thank you for what you have placed on and in my son allow him to know that his life has purpose.

In Your son Jesus Name, we pray, Amen.

Day Five

In the name of Jesus, keep a glow in his eyes and joy that springs up like a fountain! Help him to choose wisely to act and see you in everything! Jesus, you know your desires for my son's life and although he may not see it today , Lord I see in the Spirit your desire for him. Proper as your word says in **III John vs.2 – 3 – Beloved, I wish above all things that thou mayest prosper and be in health, even as thy soul prospereth. 3 For I rejoiced greatly, when the brethren came and testified of the truth that is in thee, even as thou walkest in the truth.** Allow your will to be manifested.

In Jesus Name, Amen.

Day Six

Heavenly Father, please help my son to be honest, without selfish motives, calm and able to bounce back from adversities – Let him "FEEL" the prayers sent forth on his behalf! Lord please do not turn from him even though he has turned from you, as the word says in **Ezekiel 33:9 – Nevertheless, if thou warn the wicked of his way to turn from it; if he do not turn from his way, he shall die in his iniquity; but thou hast delivered thy soul.**

This we ask in Your Son Jesus the Christ Name, Amen.

Day Seven

Please Lord, keep my son's heart pure and pining for you in his life! Hear this prayer to keep his mind stayed on His Savior and Lord, always! Lord your word says you would keep thee in perfect peace whose mind is stayed on you. As I conclude this week of prayer Lord **Psalm 42:1 says, As the heart panteth after the water brooks, so panteth my soul after thee, O God.** Pursue him Lord and allow him to pursue you and we will be forever grateful.

In Jesus Name, Amen.

Prayer for a Brother

Father (Abba) I thank you for all my brothers both natural and spiritual. I thank you for the spirit of unity that you place in them according to **Psalms 133:1**. Abba thank you for the love that is declared over him in **Hebrews 13:1.** Abba, we come into agreement with **1 John 4:20** that no hate will be among my brother but we declare **Proverbs 17:17** over him that he shall be a friend that has been proven through adversity. Abba, I thank you that I am a safe place and judgement free accountability for my brother according to **Mathew 18:15 -20**. I will listen and render righteous instruction in order to gain and retain my brother. Thank you, Abba, for providing an abundance for my brother to provide for his natural and spiritual siblings according to your word in **1 Timothy 5:8**. Abba my brother is full of word, wisdom, power and might.

This prayer is sealed in Jesus name.

Prayer on Friendship

Father I thank you for the desire to be friendly and a true friend as spoken of in **Proverbs 17:17**. Abba, for you declared that a friend is faithful & sticks closer than any brother **Proverbs 18:24**. You also declared that a pure heart and graceful speech will have the friendship of kings. **Proverbs 22:11.** Thank you Abba for friends that speak truth to me in difficult situations as **Proverb 27:5-6** states. Thank you for sending friends that sharpen me in every area of my life. Abba, thank you for the knowledge to protect my friends as they protect me as You declared in your word. I thank you for your divine design in me and for my friends to walk alongside me.

In Jesus mighty name!

BUSINESSMAN

Lord, Bless this businessman. Be his Rock and Redeemer. Thank you that you made all things, and in you all things hold together. According to **Jeremiah 29:11**, you have said that you have plans and a purpose for him, plans to prosper him not to harm him. Let him trust you with his business. May the word of Christ dwell in him richly, teaching him in all wisdom. May he work with thankfulness in his heart to God. Whatever he does, in word or deed, may he do everything in the name of the Lord Jesus, giving thanks to God the Father.

Through Jesus Christ our Lord, Amen.

Educator

Lord we pray that You would challenge the hearts of this male educator to recognize the vulnerabilities of children and to balance discipline with dignity and control with care. Help him to be conscious of the need for constructive criticism rather than destructive faultfinding and to offer a motivating environment which embraces fairness, honesty and integrity with appropriate praise, a learning environment where trust is nurtured and not exploited. Lord we pray that You would raise him up with godly standards and unbiased teaching techniques and we pray that his classroom returns to the godly principles, which our ancestors held dear.

In Jesus name we pray, Amen .

ATHLETE

Our Father, you have created us to strive for excellence in every area of our lives. Grant to all athletes, coaches, and fans, strength to pursue excellence during this event. We pray for the safety of these athletes; Protect him from injury and harm. We pray for your grace, that you would provide us with the endurance to pursue our heavenly prize: eternal life in in Christ Jesus.

Amen.

PRAYER ON MENTAL ILLNESS

Father (Abba) thank you for being with me in my darkest and most difficult time. According to your word in **Romans 8:26** the Spirit makes intercession for me. Abba, You said you're near the broken hearted and crushed spirit in **Psalms 34:18**. You reach into my darkest corners and shed light in my heart and mind according to **2 Corinthians 4:6**. Abba pull me out of the dark pit and show me light like you recorded in **Job 33:28**. Abba, You declare in **Proverbs 24:6 that in counsel you wage your war and there is safety in a multitude of counsel**. Abba, I thank you for the resources of counsel in coaches, mentors, counselors & skilled leaders. You love me and desire that I prosper even as my soul (seat of affections) prospers healthily! Amen.

FRATERNITY BROTHER

Heavenly Father blood could not make us closer. Cover my Frat as he goes about his day and his career. Allow him to be an example to other young men. Give him the strength to be a strong tower for his Sorors. Let him represent you both in word and in deed. Allow no corrupt words to proceed from his mouth. **Ephesians 4:29 says Let no corrupt communication proceed out of your mouth, but that which is good to the use of edifying, that it may minister grace unto the hearers**. Let him continue to stand by his Sorors with grace.

In Jesus Name, Amen.

Divorced Man

Father thank you for this man of God and all that life has presented him. Help him to move away from his past and move into your promise for his life. Father your word says in **Joel 2:25 that you will restore everything the locust and the cankerworm has eaten.** Restore the years of his youth. Allow him to maintain a healthy relationship with any children born of his prior marriage. Allow him to keep his heart open to love and his mind open to new opportunities.

In Jesus Name, Amen.

~PRAYERS FOR MILITARY ~
CONTRIBUTIONS NABVETS, INC. , NATIONAL VICE COMMANDER MARY ELLIOTT

Joining the Military (New Recruit)

Dear Lord, Keep the hearts and minds of ALL that honor and serve their country; help them to persevere, trust you and love you in times of loneliness and being away from families and friends. As your word says in **Psalms 91:15 - He shall call upon me, and I will answer him: I will be with him in trouble; I will deliver him, and honour him.** Father this man child has answered and accepted the duty to serve and now allow your Holy Spirit to lead and to guide him.

In Your Son Jesus Name, we Pray Amen.

Actively Serving/Deployed

Dear Lord, keep your loving arms of protection around our military soldiers. Let your Holy Spirit rest in their Soul and Minds as they perform their daily service to the fellow man without complaining! For we know there is a time for everything under the sun. The bible says in **Ecclesiastes 3:8, There is a time to love, and a time to hate; a time of war, and a time of peace.** Lord in these times, allow your peace and protection to be around him and within him.

In the Name of Jesus, the Christ, Amen.

Military Support to Fellow Comrades Deployed

Father bring bountiful blessings into the homes of those who are continuously making the grand sacrifice of serving for the Freedom of the Citizens in this Nation! For we know that all are not endowed with the courage to make the decision to serve. Father we know the man of God has been called by you, now allow him to serve and see your salvation. The bible says in, **Romans 13:4 - For he is the minister of God to thee for good. But if thou do that which is evil, be afraid; for he beareth not the sword in vain: for he is the minister of God, an avenger to execute wrath upon him that doeth evil.** Now Father we know that everything that you allowed it to take place.

In your son Jesus Name, Amen.

Returning from Deployment

Heavenly Father Protect and shield each and every soldier and veteran who has risked their lives and returned home safely. No matter when or where, thank you for shielding them Lord from the hands of the evil and wicked. May your Powerful Love embrace and heal their wounds, physically and spiritually. Thank you for allowing them to return home to their loved ones and friends. The word of God says in **Psalm 29:11, The Lord will give strength unto his people; the Lord will bless his people with peace.** We need you to be bless us with peace as they take time to reacclimate back into society. Allow those of us around them to be as empathetic as possible and to be an active part of making this transition easier.

In Jesus Christ Name, Amen.

Wounded Warriors

Abba strengthen the wounded warrior to know that Jesus understands their pain, rejection and suffering according to **Isaiah 53:3.** May their hearts be encouraged through understanding and care of those placed in their life. May the healing balm go in and soothe all doubts and anxiety. For "YOU" are more than enough!

In Christ Name, Amen.

COLLECTION OF AFFIRMATIONS

Affirmations are tools of restoration. Affirmations can be used at any time for any occasion as a reminder to your man that he is honored, valued , respected and needed.

You were created and ordained to lead;
I trust the leader in you.

There is nothing from your past that can
control your present or your future.

Your strength is amazing!

I cover you in prayer as you
make decisions for us!!

You can't FAIL!

You are resilient!

You have been crowned
with courageousness.

I trust your decision making .

I believe in YOU!

I respect and honor the Man
of God you are today.

I won't allow Corporate America to
make me challenge your masculinity.

You only WIN!!

You are valued by me.

You are freed from every generational
curse that has plagued your family.

Your seeds are freed from every generational
curse that has plagued your family.

Wealth is YOUR portion.

God will withhold nothing
GOOD from YOU.

Your life was determined before
the earth was formed.

The divorce was not your finality!!

The years that have been stolen from
you because your children were not
allowed to see you are about to be restored.
They will forgive your absence.

(ABSENT MOTHER)

Your mother's absence may have been hard, but God is supernaturally repairing the void that has been left in your life as a result of your mother's parenting choice.

Your mother's absence is no reflection of You...
Honey you have to forgive your mom and allow her to explain her reasoning for being absent.

I pray with you as you forgive your mother for her decision to be absent from your life, we trust God to guide you in the next part of your all's relation.

(Absent Father)

You are NOT your father.

Your father's absence is not a reflection
you.

Your father's absence does not predicate
what type of father you will be.

You have done an amazing job as
a father, husband and provider.

You have to forgive your father, but you
do not have to allow him to occupy space
that you are not ready to share. Give it and
yourself some time if necessary.

Abusive Parents

The abuse from your parents was
not the love that you deserved.

You were and are worthy of so
much more than they have given
to you. Allow God to demonstrate
the love you deserve through me.

I know having someone by your side to
love you and not hurt you is different but
trust the God of your soul.

I am patient with your hesitancy,
I am considerate of your pain,
I am regarding your heart.

Forgive your parents for the abuse they
caused you and for the mental dysfunction
that resulted from the abuse.

It's okay to be cautious, I pray that
it does not cause delays in the things
that God has promised you.

God through me will show you
what it means to be loved.

I will not force my love on you, I will give
you space and time to heal and seek God
for who I am in your life.

I am over here standing in prayer and
agreement for your total manifestation of
the promise.

MEN ARE NOT ALWAYS ABLE TO COMMUNICATE WHEN THEY ARE EXPERIENCING PRESSURE

It seems as though pressure has been trying to consume you, I just want you to know that my prayer and my desire for you is for the pressure to escape you. Most importantly, that it does not take you to a place that forces you to put yourself in isolation. I understand this is not something that you enjoy sharing but understand the person God has put in your life is graced for your journey. The Lord has anointed the person and prepared them to handle the pressures that life present you. You can make it, you will make it and most of all we will make it !!

I AM PUSHING YOU, WHILE GOD IS PULLING YOU

I understand that on your life's journey a lot of people turned their back on you. I also understand that on your life's journey there were people who should have been there for you, but they were not there. I want you to know that I'm not going anywhere. Also, I want you to know I am not those people! I can imagine this is scary for you and this is unchartered territory for you. But I promise you, I'm going to stand with you, I'm going to stand beside you. I'm going to believe in you. I'm going to confide in you I'm going to trust in you and whenever you think that you can't go any further, I'm going to push you. Just know baby I'm not going to push you to hurt you I'm going to push you because I see your potential. I'm going to push you because I see all that's been placed inside of you. I'm going to push you because I know that you are great, you are mighty. You are amazing and you are an overcomer and nothing from your past will control what is in your present you are not alone .

UNDERSTANDING LIFE

Life seems to be serving you a hard hand right now. As a man I am certain that this is not what you anticipated to be experiencing right now or ever for that matter. I understand that as a man your desire is to provide for your family and to make sure those that those you love have everything that they need. Baby we love you beyond your financial hiccup, we are going to lift you up and pour into you. What we want you to know is that this moment will not last forever and although it doesn't seem like it, you can see the light of day. My king, it's almost morning time for you baby. This will not be your future, and this is just a moment in your journey, this is just a bleep in your timeline.

NOTHING CAN STOP YOU

Remember nothing can stop you or prevent you from getting to the place that was ordained for you even before the foundations of the earth. If you just keep the hope, if you just keep holding on, I'm going to make sure that we make it through this storm together. I'm willing to share beans and weenies, bratwurst or filet mignon just know that it doesn't matter where we eat or what we eat. I love you for you. I love you because you have been sent into my life to be a hero , a knight, and a savior. When you get back to the place that you are headed the only thing that I want you to remember is that I never lost my respect or my hope in you.

PUT YOUR MOUTH ON HIM 30 DAY OF TEXT MESSAGE/ FACEBOOK CHALLENGE

Sending a random message of encouragement can make the entire mood of the day shift for better. Let your man know that he is not in the journey alone. Although you are physically there, it's just as important to let him know you are there mentally and spiritually as well. Take the 30-day challenge. We have provided examples of 30 days of text messages to spark your thoughts or for you to use as your daily inspiration. Remember these are not mandated, however, they are ideas that can help you and your mate open up healthy dialogues of encouragement and interactions. Please feel free to use these messages. Allow them to also be mental igniters of how to increase positive energy throughout the day.

***Please use this hashtag for Facebook.**
#putyourmouthonhim

DAY 1

When the thought of living without you crosses my
mind, my breath feels suffocated and my world spins
like a tornado!!

DAY 2

Life without you has been like a Life sentence,
without a chance of parole!

DAY 3

Your voice is my tranquility; you always make
me feel that everything will be alright.

DAY 4

Your presence is my reassurance that
Mighty Men of Valor still exist!

DAY 5

When you hold me in your arms all my
fears dissipate. Then my concerns are
no more. You Rescue me from myself.

DAY 6

PS: I've wrapped this pillow around my head smelling
your cologne and imagining you sneaking home for
lunch, lost in you…

DAY 7

Hey, may I write an excuse to your Boss ?
I need you to let me cater to you all day.

DAY 8

Take a moment baby and inhale and exhale.
We call this day blessed! We speak increased
Favor on today!! #yougotthis

DAY 9

Yes, you are the perfect one for me and my
imperfections!! You are the king of my heart.

DAY 10

God has increased your resources, remember they that wait upon the Lord, he shall renew their strength, God is renewing YOUR strength!

DAY 11

Can I do a couple of forevers with you…?

DAY 12

I want to rub you down and relax all of your muscles. Then I want to put my mouth on you. Please respond yes or no if you want me to.

DAY 13

Today is a pressing day and you have to press towards
the mark of the prize, which is in Christ Jesus.

DAY 14

Baby you don't have to get there today, just get there.
Keep your goals in front of you and I am here to cheer
for you and steer for you if you need me to.

DAY 15

I will not let you face another storm on your own.
I am here for you... No words all ears...
Imagine that, I love you baby!

DAY 16

You are my present, past and future. I don't
want to imagine life without you in it.

DAY 17

I want you to come lay in my arms and I want
to rub your head and let you know it's alright.
I just want to make you feel good all over.

DAY 18

I love how you father our children and lead our family.
You are a man after God's heart.

DAY 19

Baby when I'm with you nothing else matters.
You make my heart sing loud.

DAY 20

What's on your mind? (wait for an answer) (If he
says nothing, respond)…Can I give you something
to think about…? (give him something to arouse
him and cause him to want to get home soon.)

DAY 21

(Pick one of his physical features and tell him how
much it turns you on.) ex. I love it when you look
at me and lick your lips, it makes my body quiver.

DAY 22

(Pick something, he does that makes you feel valued)
ex. I love it when you tell me to go ahead in the house
and let you grab the bags; it makes me feel valued it.

DAY 23

I feel safe in your arms. You are
MY knight in shining armor.

DAY 24

(Pick a cologne he wears and tell him how it
arouses you) When you wear sauvage it make me
want to just seduce you as soon as you walk in the
door, I be wanting to turn the location on, on
your phone so I can stalk you.

DAY 25

How is your day? (wait for a response) (offer him
something to make it better) ex. If I picked you up
for lunch would you sneak away with me?

DAY 26

Baby please come straight home from work tonight. (if
you have kids or live ins make arrangements) We have
the house to ourselves and I want to role play with
you.(venture to spice it up)

DAY 27

WE are living in the overflow; God
is giving us more than enough.

DAY 28

Your body is the temple of God.

DAY 29

I am addicted to your touch and your smell.
They make my knees weak and my heart skip a beat.

DAY 30

I just lay in your arms and feel the warmth
of your chest and the strength of your hands.

MY PRAYER

Father we seal this book with the blood of Jesus and the Love of God.

May every woman and man who read it experience a heightened encounter in you and in their relationships.

In Jesus Name, Amen.

THE MAZE OF MARRIAGE

Before marrying my soon to be Pastor, I had a 700 plus credit score, two vehicles, money in the bank, and a heart to serve God. The pressure of others in the Ministry being married contributed to us making a premature decision to get married. I had not learned how to know if a man is a good candidate for marriage. I had already survived a prior failed marriage because I followed the guidance of the church and married to flee lust. Which resulted in marrying a drug addict and whore. I was so religious that I negated the things that mattered LOVE, HONOR, and RESPECT!! I just did not want to go to HELL for BURNING!!

Well, the second time around I, unfortunately, had not learned any more from church about marriage, nor did I venture to read a book. This time I believed it would be better because we both loved God and was serving actively in Ministry. I had become so spiritually minded I negated the obvious. Can he provide for him, you, and your daughter? How will your household be maintained? Needless to say, I mastered not having sex and failed at LIFE LESSONS. By the time the marriage began to crumble, I had lost honor and respect for my then-husband and Pastor because he could not handle the financial responsibility of the house. I began to dishonor him with my mouth. I verbally treated him in a manner unacceptable. I emasculated him on every level publicly and privately. I wounded his Spirit and stripped his drive. That was how I allowed my mouth, which was intended for other things, to be used to destroy him. The one thing that could bring us together, I enabled to form a more significant wedge in the marriage.

Once I realized I didn't know how to "Put my mouth on him" in, either way, I knew the marriage was going to dissolve. I never learned how to build him up, but I witnessed countless encounters on how to tear him down. Many women in church talk about their spouses poorly with their families and girlfriends. This same man now must face the people he has been emasculated around.

Through that divorce, I learned that I could build him up or tear him down, BUT I can't do both. For married ladies, learn to build him up because someone is waiting to take your place.

TAKE 10, TEN MINUTES TO WRITE ABOUT YOUR HUSBAND.

Take time below to write ten things you love about your mate:

1. ______________________________________

2. ______________________________________

3. ______________________________________

4. ______________________________________

5. ______________________________________

6. ______________________________________

7. ______________________________________

8. ______________________________________

9. ______________________________________

10. _____________________________________

Did you write ten things? _________ Yes or _______ No
(if no, why not?)

____

____

____

These are questions to ask yourself so that you can salvage your marriage.

Is the Love gone?________ Yes _______ No
_________ Sort of _______Unsure

If you said anything but "NO," then you have to reevaluate what has gone wrong. You have to be honest with yourself. Then be willing to PUT in the work.

List 10 things about your husband you wish you could change:

1. ____

2. ____

3. ____

4. ____

5. ____

6. ____

7. ____

8. ____

9. ____

10. ____

Ask yourself these questions:

Which list was longer?

Why do you have these feelings?

Do you want them to change?

When I realized I no longer liked my former spouse, I realized I also no longer respected him. Once the respect left, I could no longer honor him with my mouth, sexually or vocally. The marriage was in dire straits. There were plenty of examples of women in the church who loved their husband in public and shamed him offline to family and friends, why was I to be any different? That was my mindset, it was horrible, and I needed help. No one could tell me because we were the same. Could this system, designed to bring us as together as one, actually be slowly creating a hollow of divide.

I rejected him physically, mentally, and emotionally, I created the perfect place for the other woman to come in and set up a territory. So, she did and was successful. I continued to dishonor him, and the marriage continued to disintegrate. Eventually, there was no marriage; just two people cohabitating under the idea of marriage.

Marriage has to be honorable, or the other woman, which I became will honor him with the fruit of her lips verbally and sexually, and you will wonder, how did you all end up in that spot.

Married ladies take every moment to build him up; I promise life will take every chance to tear him down. And the other lady that I once was will pick up on the fact that he is vulnerable and works it to her advantage. Putting your mouth on him with positive affirmations and prayers should be done out of pure love and respect, not to prevent another from taking your mate. REMEMBER FEAR is a MAGNET. Love on him simply because you love him.

SINGLE LADIES

Ladies, please be advised building him up is a constant task, not just today, and then tomorrow, it needs to be daily. Encourage him when you can, when you feel like it, and when you don't like him too much. Learn your love language and his so you can maintain a healthy relationship via communication. Practice keeping your love life private with minimal interferences.

Things to Consider:

(Every area you critique him on you have to be equally as strong, or it is not a valid critique.)

Relationship with God	Employed
Religious affiliation	Unemployed
Credit	Children
Finances	By marriage

Outside of marriage

Criminal Record

Driving record

Extracurricular

activities

Substance abuse

(current or present)

Health

Mental Health

Debt

Residence

Education

Career

Hobbies

Animals

Transportation

Any areas not listed but a concern:

____

____

____

____

____

____

____

____

____

Ask yourself, what do I bring to the table in a
relationship?

What would I add to a man's life?

What do you want in a man?

What are you looking for in a relationship?

NOTES

NOTES

NOTES

NOTES

NOTES

NOTES

NOTES

NOTES

NOTES

NOTES

NOTES

NOTES

NOTES

NOTES

NOTES

NOTES

NOTES

NOTES

NOTES

NOTES